CW01372467

You Are Amazing

(Born to shine)

Dictionary definition:

AMAZING: causing astonishment, great wonder, awesome, excellent, fantastic, · good, great, marvellous, superb, terrifi c, very good, wonderful, stunning.

unimaginable, phenomenal, splendid, remarkable, unbe-lievable, breathtaking, tremendous, astounding, WOW!

The Bible definition:

SHINE: to stand out; You shine when you stand confi-dently in the truth of who you are! You shine when you stand confidently in your value and in the gifts you bring to the world. Jesus told us in Matthew 5:16 - Let your light shine before mankind, that they may see your good works and glorify your Father who is in Heaven.

ISBN: 978-1-9162995-6-6

Design of this book by Nancy Goudie and Chris Mathison. Series design by Helen Martin.

Cover and illustrations by Chris Mathison and Charlotte Cooke.

Published by The NGM Trust, Caedmon Complex, Bristol Road, Thornbury, BS35 3JA. www.ngm.org.uk

Printed by TJ Books, Padstow, Cornwall

Preface

Many people have told me how much they love and value these small hardbacked books as gifts for themselves and also as gifts for their friends and family. Each book is designed to be opened at any page when you feel discouraged and what you read will bring encouragement for your soul. I have written six of these books. They are called, The Beloved, Confident? You Are Special, You Are Beautiful, You Are Loved and now You Are Amazing. I have loved writing each one. As I have said before this is not a book you read from cover to cover, but a book you can pick up at any time and find encouragement and food for your soul. Pick it up and read the words contained therein and experience an explosion of joy in your heart.

Each of us deserves to know the truth about who we are!

We live in a world full of negativity and we so often believe and agree with the words spoken against us. But this is not who we are! We all need to know that we are incredible, wonderful, beautiful, significant and amazing!

Inside this book (like the others) you will discover stories, songs, quotes, prophetic words and Bible verses that will speak into the deepest places of our hearts and minds. I am praying that the words of this book will reach you at your lowest points as well as the highest planes of your life, to bring you more joy and help you to discover your life being filled with much encouragement, brilliance and revelation.

I am praying you will see that you shine in the darkness and the light that is within you declares to the world that each of us is unique and special.

Pick up this book at any time, turn to any page and you will find that kind of encouragement and comfort for your soul. It will give you what you need in the midst of sorrow, grief and pain but also what you need when you are briming with life and laughter. Never forget you are amazing and you were born to shine!

YOU ARE AMAZING

(Born to shine)

In case no one has told you lately, you are

amazing, strong, brave, wonderful, kind, loved, worthy,

and there is no one like you.
The world needs you.
- *Unknown*

Learn to love the real YOU!

You Are:

Stunning
Phenomenal
Remarkable
Breathtaking
Tremendous
Beautiful and
Simply Amazing!

On a scale from 1 to 10, you are an 11

This is what the Lord says - he who made you and formed you in the womb, and who will help you, *"Do not be afraid, for I have chosen you."* (Isaiah 44:2)

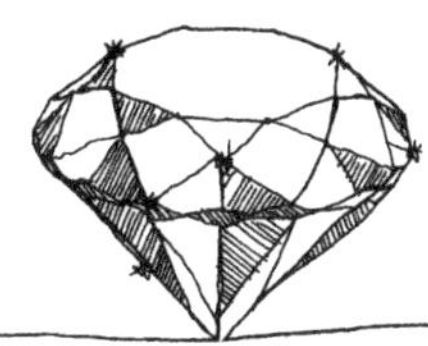

This book is designed to encourage you and inform you that you are amazing.

Often in life comments from others can bring you down and destroy the passion to believe that you are amazing. The truth is that you are incredible. I wonder how many times a day you get told that you are wonderful, that you will be successful in life, that the plans for your life are huge and so very interesting. We all need encouragement but I wonder how many people receive it.

I hope what I am about to write encourages you to not believe the negatives you hear and not take on board the rejection and significant doubt you may receive.

Many incredible and successful people were told that they would not amount to anything in their lives. People like:

Walt Disney,
Michael Jordon
Albert Einstein
Vincent Van Gough
Oprah Winfrey
Steve Jobs

All of them received rejection early in their lives/careers.

Walt Disney was fired from a newspaper job for 'lacking imagination' and having no good ideas. He was also initially told that a cartoon mouse would never work!

Michael Jordon was cut from his high school basketball team and early in his NBA career he faced criticism.

Albert Einstein was given a letter from his teacher and was told to give it to his mother. He asked his mother what it said and she replied: "Your son is a genius. This school is not advanced enough and doesn't have enough good teachers to teach him. Please teach him yourself." She did teach him herself, but Einstein discovered later that she had lied. He found the same note many years later and the note actually read: 'Your son is mentally deficient. We cannot let him attend our school anymore. He is expelled.'

Vincent Van Gogh died penniless and destitute believing himself to be an artistic failure. He only sold one painting in his life and that was to a friend for a small amount of money. But in the century after his death, he became perhaps the most recognised painter of all time.

Oprah Winfrey was told she wasn't fit for television news. She faced failure many times, but never gave up!

Steve Jobs was fired from the company he created. He was expelled from school and was bullied in middle school. He was not wanted by his birth parents.

All these people received huge setbacks, but achieved massive things in their lives even though many people didn't see their potential or realise they had incredible gifts.

I'm glad I'm me!

So many of us never think we are amazing! Others seem more likeable, more interesting, more educated, more informed, more talented and gifted than we could ever be. We often wish we were more like someone else that we admire.

My husband was a very talented man who wrote musicals, spoke on public platforms and had many of his songs published, yet he often wished he was more gifted like others he admired. One day after spending some time reading the Bible and praying to God, he burst into our bedroom where I was busy getting dressed and sat on our bed. He said,

I looked at him in astonishment and waited to hear what else he wanted to say! He repeated himself and said, *"I'm glad I'm me"* and then went on to say:

"I don't want to be Andrew Lloyd Webber. I don't want to be Billy Graham! I don't want to be anyone else! I'm glad I'm me. I'm glad God made me, me with all the gifts God has given me. I love my creativity! I love what I get to do every day! I don't want to be anyone else! I'm glad I'm me!"

Are you aware of how special and amazing you are?

Are you **glad** you are you?

Be yourself; everyone else is already taken.

Oscar Wilde

Be your amazing self and enjoy life to the full

Life is meant to be lived fully with peace and joy!

(John 10:10; John 14:27; John 15:11)

Gladness and joy will overtake you and sorrow and sighing will flee away.

(Isaiah 55:11) 

joy

In case I haven't told you before or you have not heard clearly enough -

you are unique,
phenomenal,
remarkable,
breathtaking
and totally awesome!

What a beauty you are!

Woohoo!

You're amazing **just the way you are.**

Bruno Mars

Amazing

Are you allowing your negative thoughts to destroy the truth of who you are?

If you feel broken, overlooked, ignored, small, weary, heartbroken, misunderstood or rejected......
remember the truth about who you are!

Turn your thoughts to good thoughts, to kind words, to truth - you are precious, you are awesome, you are strong, you are beautiful and you are brave!
Remember the truth about who you are!

YOU ARE AWE-INSPIRING!
Believe the truth about who you are!

Just Believe!

THE BLESSING

A song you may remember which was released around the world during the Covid pandemic was called The Blessing……here are the words to remind you:

The Lord bless you and keep you
Make His face shine upon you and be gracious to you
The Lord turn His face toward you
And give you peace

The Lord bless you and keep you
Make His face shine upon you and be gracious to you
The Lord turn His face toward you
And give you peace

Amen, amen, amen

The Lord bless you and keep you
Make His face shine upon you and be gracious to you
The Lord turn His face toward you
And give you peace

Amen, amen, amen

May His favour be upon you
And a thousand generations
And your family and your children
And their children, and their children

May His presence go before you
And behind you, and beside you
All around you, and within you
He is with you, he is with you

In the morning, in the evening
In your coming, and your going
In your weeping, and rejoicing
He is for you, he is for you
He is, He is

Amen, amen, amen
Amen,

Source: Musixmatch. Songwriters: Chris Brown / Steven Furtick / Cody Carnes / Kari Brooke Jobe. The Blessing lyrics © Worship Together Music, Capitol Cmg Paragon, Be Essential Songs, Kari Jobe Carnes Music, Writers Roof Publishing

Find this song online, play it and allow the blessing from the Lord to pour down on your life again and again!

This song came from a portion of the Bible which says:

The Lord bless you and keep you
The Lord make his face to shine upon you and be gracious to you
The Lord turn his face toward you and give you peace
(Numbers 6:24-26)

This is another great blessing to read over your life regularly.

This is how God sees you - his amazing and beautiful child.

- Do you not know how perfectly you have been made?
- Do you not know how wonderfully special you are?
- You are crafted to perfection even in the smallest detail.
- You are beautiful from head to toe, beautiful beyond compare; absolutely flawless.
- Your beauty shines like the sun in the sky! (Whether male or female you are indeed beautiful.)

- Receive the love and grace being poured out on you.
- Receive the oil of joy as I pour it upon your soul.
- Let the perfume of my love soak into your mind.
- Receive the fragrance of my smile, let it penetrate deep within.
- Take what is rightfully yours.
- Let my words bring you deep healing as I pour these oils and perfumes upon you.

- I want you to know there is much ahead for you.
- There are treasures beyond belief.
- There's an inheritance of good things stored up for you.
- Keep looking. Keep searching, keep asking and listening and good things will come to you.

- There are many treasures stored up for you.
- Open your heart and receive them now.
- Stand underneath the fountain of blessing and be drenched in love.

YOU ARE SIMPLY **amazing!**

If someone asked me to describe you in just 2 words, I'd say...simply **amazing**

UNKNOWN

You are **amazing**, you are **important**, you are **special**, you are **unique**, you are **precious**, you are **loved.**

UNKNOWN

You are the **only version** of you to ever exist in the universe. You are **great**, you are **powerful**, you are **special**.

UNKNOWN

You were born to shine

10 ways to shine

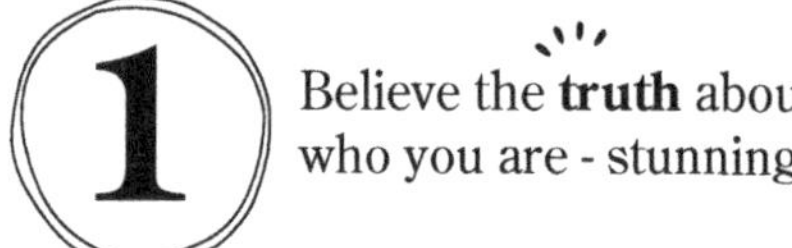

1 Believe the **truth** about who you are - stunning!

2 **Smile** - your smile is amazing! Smile even when life is hard – a smile can change the way you feel and also provide you with an instant facelift.

3 Learn to **sing** - Sing and believe the truth of who you are! Singing improves your health, your breathing, relieves stress and even burns calories!

4 Your **passion** - display your passion through your words and deeds. Let your emotions out – don't imprison them within you.

Your **values** - learn to treat everyone the way you would like to be treated.

Keep a **gratitude** journal and review it regularly. Gratitude improves your mental health and reduces anxiety and stress.

Display **confidence** even when you feel those butterflies in your tummy! They are there to remind you that your strength comes from above!

Learn to **love** the unlovely - each one of us is precious and deeply loved by God.

Care for those who need a kind word or deed. Tell them they are phenomenal!

Shine in the darkness and in the light. You shine when you stand confidently knowing who you are!

You are AMAZING!

To shine means to radiate peace, hope and joy even in the middle of difficult times.

As you dance, sing, worship - let your light shine and you will draw all people to see the light.
Shine through your attitude, words and deeds.

Remember you are awesome!

For God who said,

"Let light shine out of darkness, made his light shine in our hearts to give us the light of the knowledge of the glory of God in the face of Christ."
(2nd Corinthians 4:6)

Do everything without complaining or arguing so that you may become blameless and pure children of God without fault in a crooked and depraved generation in which you shine like stars in the universe."
(Philippians 2:14-15)

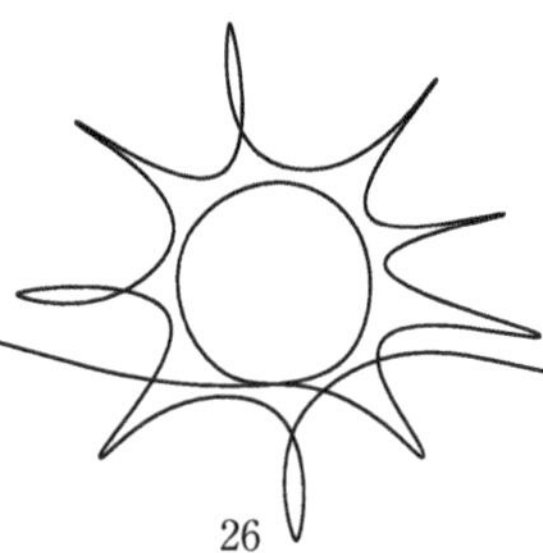

Do you know that:

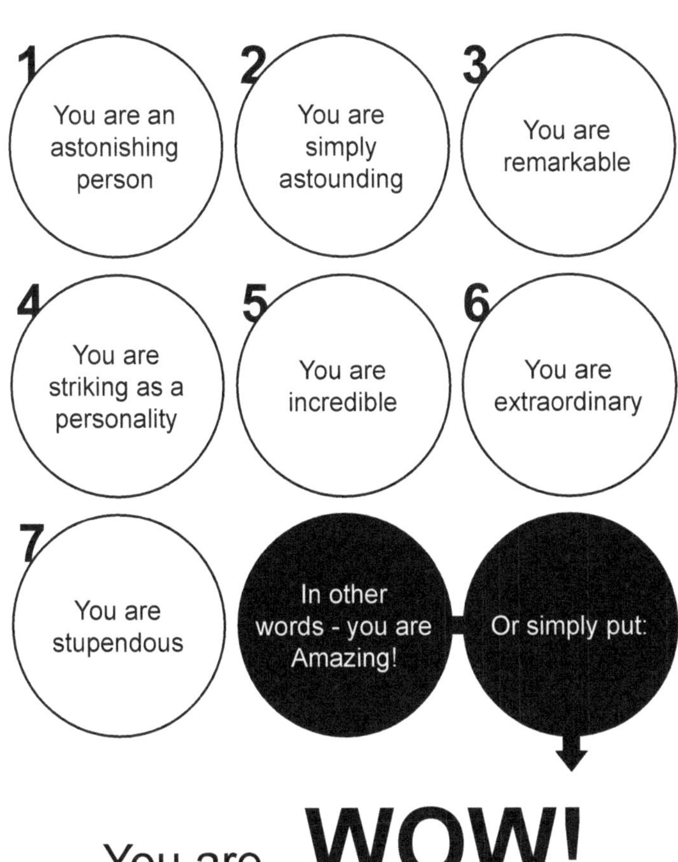

You are - **WOW!**

YOU ARE INDESCRIBABLE!

There are not enough words to describe the creator who made you in your mother's womb!

We were made in the image of God who is indescribable! He is amazing and therefore we are amazing!

How do we know that our creator is indescribable? Well.....look outside on a dark night and look up at the stars! Look at pictures taken of our universe – or read about what is in our universe! The Bible says the heavens display the glory of God. Day after day they speak and night after night they tell us what they know. The stars are declaring that our creator is indescribable. He is amazing and therefore because we are made in his image - we too are amazing!

We live in the Milky Way galaxy and our sun is a million times bigger than the earth. You can fit one million three hundred thousand earths into our sun! It's huge and yet it is only one star in a billion stars in our galaxy. In the known universe there are about two trillion galaxies. Wow! If we were to see a picture of the universe our sun would be so small that you would not be able to see it. You can now understand how small we are in comparison.

Our God is huge and although we are so small, he loves and values us.

The Bible says he calls each of the stars in the universe by name, and the truth is he calls each of us by name too. Have you ever heard him call your name? Listen in the quietness and hear the voice of God whispering your name! He is kind, compassionate, loving and he knows you are amazing! Never shortchange yourself! You are incredible.

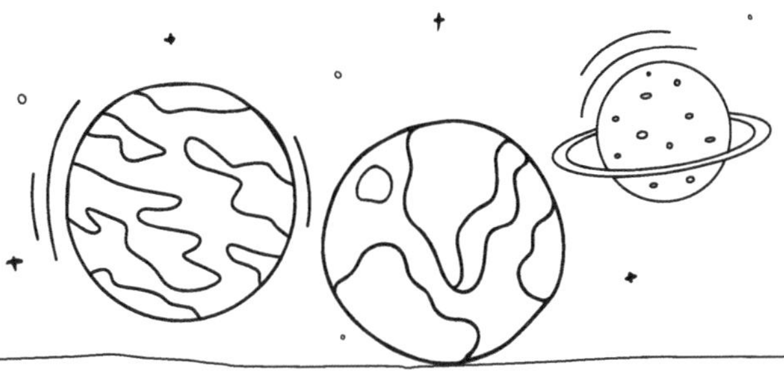

Know
the
truth
and
let
the
truth
set
you
free

(Jesus speaking in John 8:32)

I know from experience that when negative comments are spoken to you and you believe them it causes you to see the world you live in from that frame of mind.

I heard about a guy who was told he was not very clever when he was five years old. Throughout the years despite the good grades he got and the scholarships he received, those words from his teacher remained with him.

We need to remember that our words **are powerful.**

He told a story of a woman who was conducting an experiment on several adults. She told them that she was going to cause them to have scars on their faces and it would be achieved by really good make up.

When this was done she brought in a hand held mirror because there were no mirrors in the room. She individually showed them what they looked like. You can imagine what a shock it was to see their faces so scarred.

Then she told them that she was going to do something to their scars that would mean that the scars could not be removed. In actual fact what she did was to remove the scars, but the people did not realise that.

She then told them to go to a different part of the building and mix with people who were there and tell her how they were received by others. They all came back saying that the people they spoke to were not nice to them and that they couldn't stop staring at their scars.

You see the words spoken to us show us the world **through a different frame.**

They believed they had scars so ugly that people would react negatively to them.

In fact there were no scars there at all. The scars had been removed but because they had been told that the scars were permanently on their faces, they believed the words spoken to them.

How many times do we believe the words spoken to us or about us?

Let's **listen to the truth** and reject the lies, because the truth will indeed **set us free.**

An Act of Kindness that led to a miracle!

Imagine a humble Scottish farmer named Fleming toiling away on his farm, when suddenly, piercing screams shatter the tranquillity. Without a second thought, he abandons his tools and races towards the distress. What he finds is a child struggling in the swamp, trapped and drowning. With no hesitation, Fleming risks his own life, using a long branch to pull the child to safety.

The very next day, a luxurious car pulls up to Fleming's modest home. Out steps a distinguished gentleman - Randolph Churchill, the father of the boy Fleming saved. Churchill offers to repay the farmer's bravery with riches, but Fleming refuses, saying, **"Saving someone is my duty; humanity has no price."**

Just then, Fleming's own son appears at the door. Churchill, intrigued, asks, **"Is this your son?"** When Fleming proudly confirms, Churchill proposes an intriguing deal: if Fleming won't accept his money, he'll fund the boy's education at the finest schools, ensuring he gets the same opportunities as Churchill's own child.

Fleming, realizing the chance to give his son a future he could never afford, gratefully accepts. His son goes on to attend St Mary's Medical School in London and becomes Sir Alexander Fleming, the inventor of penicillin.

But here's where the story comes full circle: years

later, it is penicillin that saves the life of Winston Churchill, Randolph's son, who would become the Prime Minister of Britain twice.

Isn't it fascinating how a single act of kindness can ripple through history, connecting lives in such unexpected ways?

Amazing!

I read this story recently and although I had read it before, I felt it was important to put it in this book.

We live in a world where kindness is often forgotten.

We see an injustice, but we do not act.

We read a horrible comment on Facebook and sometimes add another unkind comment to the trail of words.

We need to shine our light by being kind, loving, faithful and doing our duty to others around us.

Every day let's add an act of kindness to our actions!

Perhaps this story will show you how our God can use a simple act of kindness in a phenomenal way!

Lord...........

You made my whole being; you formed me in my mother's body. I praise you because you made me in an amazing and wonderful way. What you have done is astounding. I know this very well. You saw my bones being formed as I took shape in my mother's body. All the days planned for me were written in your book before I was one day old.

Paraphrase of Psalm 139:14-16

AMAZING!!

Even when you don't have a dream for your life **GOD ALWAYS DOES.**

In the 80's and 90's we trained many people in their teens and twenties who were creatives in the musical arts. We would, at times, invite others to come and teach our students. One of the things they often asked them was *"What is your dream?"* After these sessions, I remember one person saying to me, *"I don't like these sessions because I don't have a dream. Everyone has a dream and I don't, so I never know what to say."*

> I told the person who spoke with me. *"Don't worry. You are only in your teens, you may not have a dream, but God has a dream and a plan for your life. Ray and I were in our late twenties when God revealed his dream for our lives. He called us into full time Christian work. We moved to England and started a band. We played to packed audiences in halls and theatres all over the UK and appeared on TV and Radio. We had a hit in the top 40 and played on Top of the Pops! We saw thousands of lives transformed and miracles, sheer miracles happened! God's dream for our lives came into being. I didn't know God's dream for us until I was in my mid-twenties. I never dreamt that dream – it was God's dream. I just said YES. If you don't have a dream for your life – please don't worry, just relax and say "Yes" to whatever God has for you, because his dream for your life is amazing – beyond all you could ask or imagine!"*

God knows who you are. God knows you are amazing! His plan and dream for your life is so good.

Just say **YES!**

We were created in the image of God (Genesis 1:27) ......so we are like him!

He is totally and utterly amazing and therefore we too are......

Amazing!

Song of Love

The two brothers could not be more different. The older one had everything! He was clever; confident, was blessed with good looks, had lots of friends and had everything going for him. The younger brother was not clever, or good looking, in fact he had a hunchback and very few friends. He was not confident; however, he had an amazing singing voice. He used to fill the house with songs of joy.

When the brothers were at boarding school, the older brother did not want anyone to know that the boy with the hunchback was his younger brother. One day the brother with the wonderful voice was picked upon by some boys at his school. They called him names and ripped off his shirt to expose his deformed back. The older brother, who was an admired leader of the student body knew what was happening but choose not to intervene. The younger boy felt betrayed by his brother by what he failed to do. He left the school and from that day on he never sang again.

Years passed and the subject of that day was never spoken about. One day the older brother realised what he had done. He was full of remorse and travelled hundreds of miles to come home and beg his brother's forgiveness. The two brothers talked long into the night and they hugged and cried together as forgiveness flowed. During the night the older brother awoke to the sound of beautiful singing which flooded the house. His younger brother was singing again.

It's amazing what love and forgiveness will do!

Amazing what love can do!

I heard a story a while ago about a pastor who could not cope with the stress and strain of life. The pressures upon his life were so strong that one day he left his church, his job, his home, his family, friends and his wife! He travelled by himself to a remote place in the mountains where he stayed in a little cabin. The only heat came from a very small electric fire. One day as he huddled around his little fire feeling very low, the electric heater died. It was the last straw! He kicked the electric heater in disgust and shouted at the top of his voice, *"I hate you God."* He then sank to his knees sobbing. As he was crying, he heard the voice of God say gently, *"I know and I understand."* He then heard Jesus sobbing with him.

When he heard Jesus sobbing, he got up on his feet, dried his eyes and got into his car. He drove back home to the same situation with the same problems, but he knew he could cope because he knew Jesus loved him and he was with him.

When you know how much you are loved by the most amazing God of all creation and that he never leaves us alone, you can cope much better with the stresses of life.

The Lord himself goes before you and will be with you; he will never leave you nor forsake you. Do not be afraid; do not be discouraged.

(Deuteronomy 31:8)

You are Amazing!

Remember that **always!**

You Are *Never* Forgotten!

Do you at times feel abandoned?
Do you feel naked and left on your own?
Do you feel forsaken?
Do you feel left out and alone?
Are you broken hearted?

THEN

Remember *your value!*
Remember *you are loved beyond all measure!*
Remember *you are never on your own!*
Remember *God is close to the broken hearted*
and *he brings comfort to those who feel forsaken.*

You Are Special and you are *never* forgotten!

(Isaiah 49:15)

Like the stars in the sky
you shine and always
make your mark.

○ You Are **Unique**

○ You are **Incredible**

○ You are **Amazing!**

○ You are **Beautiful**

Don't listen to the negative voices in you or around you! They don't speak with love for love is kind, it is not rude, it is not proud. It doesn't envy and does not delight in evil. **Instead** rejoice in the truth of who you are:

You are awesome - one of a kind
There is no one quite like you!
You truly are incredible!

The world is so much more beautiful with you in it!

How do you start your day

- [ ] Cursing the alarm?

- [ ] Tired, wishing you didn't need to get up?

- [ ] Dreading the day ahead?

- [ ] Turning on the news and letting it confirm your worst fears that the world is going nuts?

- [ ] You wake realising this is a new fresh day with loads of possibilities

- [ ] You spend the first portion of your day reading, watching or listening to something positive and motivational

☐ You write at least three things in your gratitude journal that you are grateful for...... even if it is that you had a bed to sleep on and air in your lungs.

☐ You realise that the kind of day you are going to have relies on your positive outlook on life, so you feed yourself with good things and avoid negative words from yourself or others.

☐ You focus on your goals for this day realising that you can do more when you have a positive outlook in life.

☐ You pray and ask for help with your day.........

At the end of the day:

You reflect on your day and write down your gratitude for the help you received and for the tasks you completed.

Always Remember................

You are amazing and it is always possible for you to have an amazing day but the way you start each new day obviously helps you to enjoy this gift *(yes, that's the right word)* - this gift of a new day! **Tomorrow is never guaranteed.**

So, enjoy each new and precious day!

12 things

1. The past can't be changed, but you can change your future.
2. Opinions don't define your reality - the truth is you are awesome.
3. Everyone's journey is different - don't compare yourself with everyone else.
4. Love others as you love yourself.
5. Overthinking will lead to sadness - rest your mind and be restored.
6. Happiness is found within - rejoice and again I say rejoice.
7. Your thoughts affect your mood - do not be anxious about anything instead pray about everything!

to remember:

8 Smiles are contagious - and not only light up a room but light you up on the inside too.

9 Kindness is free - one of the flavours of the fruit of the Spirit.

10 It's okay to let go and move on - leave everything in the arms of God.

11 Cast all your anxieties on the Lord, for he cares for you!

12 When you hand problems and difficulties over to God - he will bring good from even the most difficult situation.

Things that show you are AMAZING

You are beautiful inside and out
You are thoughtful and notice the little things
You are not afraid of asking for help
You listen like it's the last conversation you will ever have
You make other people feel valued
You are able to forgive
You are kind

Remember..................................

You are Astonishing!

You are Incredible!

You are Amazing!

Has anyone ever
told you that you are
breath-taking!

Well, **it's true**
you are extremely
beautiful, talented
and amazing!

Relax and enjoy being
who you are!

Amazing

Talented

This
is who *you are!*

You are loved beyond all measure
You are beautiful inside and out
You are incredible and so greatly honoured
You are held whether you feel it or not
You are protected from all harm
Nothing and no one can harm you
You are surrounded by love and grace

You are adored
This is who you are!

The Bible says that you are **fearfully and wonderfully made**, created in the image of God. He formed you in your mother's womb, and he knows you inside and out.

Do you realise that he has...

Numbered the hairs on your head,

He knows you so intimately,

you are God's masterpiece, and

He, the one who knows everything, knows that you are...

AMAZING

Amazing grace, how sweet the sound
That saved a wretch like me
I once was lost, but now I'm found
Was blind, but now I see

'Twas grace that taught my heart to fear
And grace my fears relieved
How precious did that grace appear
The hour I first believed
Through many dangers, toils, and snares
We have already come
'Twas grace that brought us safe thus far
And grace will lead us home

When we've been there ten thousand years
Bright shining as the sun
We've no less days to sing God's praise
Than when we've first begun
Than when we've first begun

Written by John Newton © Public Domain

This is a hymn that was originally written as a poem in 1772 by John Newton. Before he was an Anglican minister John Newton participated in the slave trade and had captained a slave ship that brought slaves to the shores of the UK. He experienced God's grace and mercy for what he had done and it changed him forever.

The hymn *"Amazing Grace"* was inspired, in part by the author's real-life experiences of receiving God's grace despite having done terrible things in his life. This hymn has been sung all over the world by millions of people. We too can receive God's amazing grace when we come with a sorry heart for the things we have done wrong.

Let the words of this hymn speak to you as you read them. Let them remind you of how special and amazing you are and how wonderful God's grace is to each of us!

I heard an amazing story recently about George Washington before he became President of the United States.

He was a courier for an English General called Braddock during the French and Indian war. All the other couriers were killed. George Washington had two horses shot from beneath him. He had four bullet holes in his jacket but no flesh wounds. He had bullet fragments in his hair but no flesh wounds. Many years later before he became president, he was back in that same area. One of the Indian chiefs who had been involved was elderly at this point and near death therefore asked his braves, *"Take me to see this man. I must see him before I die."* They took him and he spoke with Washington. He told him *"Sir I am an expert marksman and I shot you 17 times and my men shot you too. After a while I told my men – Stop wasting your bullets! And I just wanted to meet the man who was protected by the great Presence above."*

The man who told this story said that this incredible story used to be in all the History books until it became politically incorrect. Why was it politically incorrect? The answer was because it mentioned God.

This is a story which should be told all the world over.

This story is Amazing

God is Amazing

Our great bodyguard

Many celebrities and members of the Royal Family have bodyguards to protect them and keep them from harm. Did you know that you have a bodyguard? ***The best one ever!***

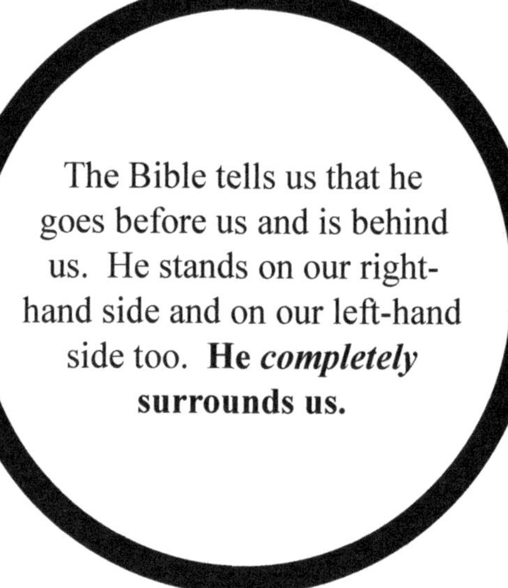

If you are a Christian then he lives inside you and you live inside of him. What a bodyguard. ***The best ever!***

The powerful creator of the universe is your protector. No matter what you go through - remember you have the best bodyguard loving and protecting you.

God will be your bodyguard to protect you when trouble is near.

(Psalm 34:20 TPT)

Don't ever forget how
incredible, gorgeous,
stunning, precious and
wonderful you are. You are.......

...........simply amazing and
you were born to shine!!

About the Author

Nancy Goudie is a well-known speaker and author. She and her late husband formed the band Heartbeat in the 80's and went on to found NGM and The Inspire Arts Trust based at Caedmon (their multi-million-pound arts and music complex). Nancy has written 20 books and recorded 6 meditation CD's and 2 Bible/Prayer CD's. She has also founded Nancy Goudie's Spiritual Health Weekends for women in the UK in luxury hotels. These weekends are like no other where everyone who attends feels special from the moment they arrive. She also holds Spiritual Health Days and Retreats in various parts of the UK and beyond. She is regularly on TV/ Radio and has developed her own podcast plus a new online programme for men and women. Nancy speaks at conferences, events and churches in various parts of the world.

For more information on Nancy's ministry or to book her to come to your area, please visit:

www.nancygoudie.com
or www.ngm.org.uk

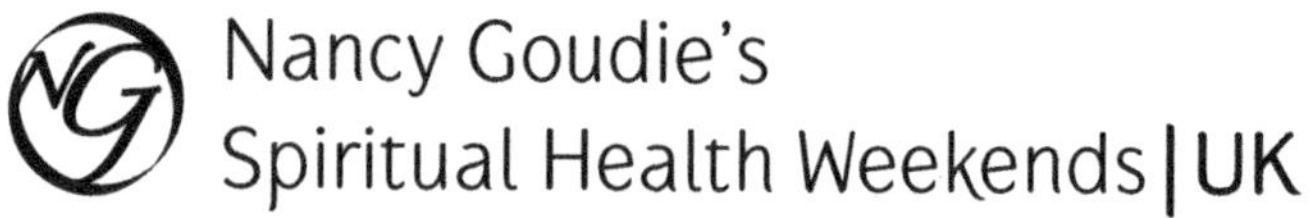

One life changing weekend in a stunning 4-star hotel!

This is a weekend like no other. It's a place for women of all ages to be pampered physically yet toned up spiritually at the same time. You will feel special from the moment you arrive to the moment you leave! Come and see for yourself what this wonderful, spectacular and unique weekend is all about. This is a God appointment for you!

Nancy Goudie has been running these luxury, unique and sensational weekend conferences for many years in 4-star luxury hotels in the UK. Why not join Nancy for: Nancy's inspiring and life-changing teaching, powerful and intimate worship from the ngm worship band, inspiring input from special guests, pampering experiences, 5 star entertainment, special individual words from God, creative optional sessions, a God perfumed prayer room and so much more!

Worried you can't afford the cost? Talk to us about spreading your payments. You can also apply for a subsidised place through our bursary scheme.

Don't miss out! This is a precious God appointment for you!

What people say:

"There is nothing else like this, it's wonderful." **J.H**

"I felt God tell me that it was a privilege to attend these weekends. When I came to the first one many years ago, the love and care I felt then is still as strong 15 years later!" **SS**

"The Spiritual Health Weekends are better than a holiday in Disneyland - I just knew I had to be there this year" **SR**

For more information and booking details

visit www.nancygoudie.com or call 01454 414880

Nancy Goudie's Spiritual Health Retreats | UK

4 days/3 nights in stunning British countryside. One in Devon and one in the Lake District.

All Accommodation has Hot Tubs.

I want to invite you to a very special, beautiful retreat in the stunning British countryside. These beautiful cottages both in Devon and in the Lake District are complete with their own hot tubs, plus amazing leisure facilities and a spa are available in a complex on the resort (Devon resort). Set in stunning countryside, this is the perfect place to relax and be revived. These amazing retreats are only for a small amount of people.

"I am so excited about these Spiritual Health Retreats! Every conference I run, God transforms lives and does miracles, and these retreats are no different. They are a place to rest, relax and enjoy the beautiful surroundings and facilities, but they will also be a place where we can explore with a small group of people, the incredible love of God for each one of us. At both retreats we have sessions with intimate worship and inspiring teaching. Plus we have our Health and Wellbeing sessions as part of these retreats too.

We will have some optional walks and optional fitness sessions and enjoy eating together at least once.

There will be optional extras you can have including extra meals, spa treatments and optional activities as well, details of which will be available nearer the time. I would love you to join me"

Nancy x

"Got so much from this time away... thank you for a wonderful experience. God was so present!!! Loved each session... Nancy is inspirational... The attention to detail phenomenal. So, so wonderful. Thanks for everything" Delegate

"Just feel so blessed this weekend in so many ways. Just thank you doesn't seem to be anywhere near enough for how I feel – so blessed by you and thank you for such an opportunity to step out of the madness into such a relaxing space." Delegate

For more information and booking details contact Zoe Wickham at:

NGM, Caedmon Complex, Bristol Road, Thornbury, Bristol BS35 3JA
Tel: 01454 414880 **Email:** zoewickham@ngm.org.uk
Or visit: www.nancygoudie.com

Other Paperback Books and Products

by Nancy Goudie. Available at www.nancygoudie.com

You Are Loved

The Beatles told us in the 1960's 'all we need is love' yet so many of us still don't know what real love feels like. Many of us have experienced a love which has scarred us because it was less than true love should be. We often yearn for someone to truly love us. This book shows that you are beautifully loved and cherished. We are all born with a longing to be loved yet sometimes we feel that no one truly loves us. Yet this is so far from the truth.

If you wake up feeling miserable, unloved and life feels hard then open this book at any page and you will receive encouragement for your soul. You will read about a love that is there for you no matter what is happening in your world. The truth is that you are valued, deeply loved, cherished and protected. This book shows you how wonderful you are!

Who Would Ever Have Thought

This is the incredible story of two ordinary people from Ayr in Scotland. They lived in an idyllic and beautiful bungalow, had terrific jobs as well as a brand new sporty car, had a myriad of wonderful friendships and brilliant families too, but they left it all behind to follow God on what turned out to be an amazing faith filled journey. It's the story of Heartbeat, ngm, Caedmon – their £3 million pound arts facility, Nancy's Spiritual Health Weekends, Ray's musicals luv esther, The Prodigals and much, much more. Nancy takes you through the highs as well as the lows, yet once you've finished reading, you'll be left feeling encouraged and built up. There are many places where you will laugh and a few where you may shed a tear! This is not just a story; this is a journey that will change your life. **Also available on Amazon Kindle and audiobook (via Audible)**

Spiritual Health Encounters

This unique and creative book helps you to spend time in the secret place and will transform and deepen your intimacy with God. Each practical exercise takes you on an exciting, creative journey of mediation, hearing from heaven, writing a psalm and real encounters with God. It's great for individuals, small groups and for counsellors/disciplers to give to those who need to see a breakthrough. This is a dynamic book that can really change lives! **Also available on Amazon Kindle.**

You Are Beautiful (hardback book)

The title of this book says it all – You Are Beautiful – Born to be Significant. Whether you are a man or a woman we are all unique, creative, wonderful, significant, valuable, and yes beautiful human beings. We all need to know how incredible we are. Each one of us was born with beauty and creativity in our DNA because each of us whether male or female was born in the image of God (Genesis 1:27). We have all been put on this planet for a purpose and a reason and therefore the truth is all of us have been born to be significant.

This book is designed to encourage and bless you. If one day you wake up feeling miserable, or at any point in the day you get a knock back from a comment someone has said about you, then pick up this book. Open it at any page and you will receive encouragement for your soul. You will hear the truth about who you are and no matter what anyone else thinks or says, you are born to be significant, and you are a wonderful, creative, beautiful human being.

Treasures of Darkness

This is a very naked and honest autobiographical account of a time when the world around Nancy started to collapse. Her husband, Ray, fell into a dark pit where he experienced ill health and burnout. At the same time God was taking their ministry, ngm, through a shift, which caused much pain and insecurity and led to many people eventually leaving. Pressures swept in like a storm leaving devastation, confusion and unanswered prayers. Nancy discovered that through this time there were *'treasures of darkness and riches hidden in a secret place'* (Isaiah 45:3).

Confident? (hardback book)

This book is for anyone who sometimes swings from being confident to feeling a failure. It's a book full of encouragement, wise words, poems, songs and stories to lift your spirit and get you back on your feet again, ready to face life once more. Through its pages you will feel accepted, really loved and realise afresh how amazing you are!

You are Special (hardback book)

In our culture of stress with so much pressure to look good and be famous, we often need to be reminded just how unique, precious, remarkable and extraordinary we are! No matter what colour our skin is, what size we are, what intelligence we display, what background we come from, the truth is each of us is an exceptional human being. In every page of this book you will discover the truth about yourself and realise afresh that you are deeply loved, special and accepted.

Oasis of Hope (hardback book)

There are times in our lives when we all need an oasis, a place where we can go and receive a thirst quenching drink for our souls. This book is such a place! A place where hope is renewed and faith can begin to grow. A place that will help refresh the reader physically, mentally, emotionally and spiritually. A place that gives us more of what we need to enable us to keep on going in our journey through life. It is designed to plant seeds of hope into the barren places of our hearts and encourage those seeds to grow and develop so that our faith will soar.

Oasis of Delight (hardback book)

There are times in our lives when we need an oasis, a place where we can go to receive a thirst quenching drink for our souls. This book is an exploration of what it means to live in the oasis of delight, tasting its fruit, relaxing and relishing in the lush surroundings; free to explore and enjoy the depths of his fulness of joy and his pleasures forevermore. It inspires us to enjoy the delightful fruit of intimacy with God, whilst all the time pointing us towards the day when we will be in the ultimate garden of delight for eternity.

The Best Is Yet To Come Journal (hardback)

This fantastic journal has a page of inspiration from Nancy and plenty of pages for your notes, prayers, drawings etc. Printed with a luxury finish this is the ideal journal for you – grab your copy now.

Our Greatest Adventure

This book tells a story of courage in the midst of pain, peace in the midst of sorrow and trust in the midst of confusion. It's a story of love and devotion in the midst of one of the biggest challenges Ray and Nancy Goudie have ever known. It's the story of God's faithfulness when Ray was diagnosed as having pancreatic cancer and of God's continued faithfulness and immense presence when Ray walked through the valley of the shadow of death and eventually fell asleep into the arms of Jesus. This is an honest, deep and raw story that will touch your emotions, making you laugh as well as cry. There are many funny and humorous moments amidst the pain and the heartache. It's a story that will fuel your faith in God and ignite your passion for his presence. This is a story that many have said had to be told. **Also available on Amazon Kindle.**

All books are available direct from ngm at:
www.ngm.org.uk, www.nancygoudie.com

Meditation CDs

Smile

If you are feeling the daily stresses of life, the busyness of work, the pressures of family or just need some soothing for your soul, then this is recording for you. **Also available to download from iTunes and other online platforms.**

Meditations for the Beloved

We all need to know we are loved and valued. This incredible music and medi-ation CD will take you to the secret place where you will know you are The Beloved; you will be overwhelmed with love, feel accepted and experience a peace that passes all understand-ing. **Also available to download from iTunes and other online platforms.**

Speak...Declare the Truth: Vol 1

Are you feeling overwhelmed? Are circum-stances or people getting you down? Are you in need of encouragement? Do you need to know you are loved? Do you need to see a mir-acle of health or provision? Does everything seem impossible for you? Then I have news for you! The Bible says in 2 Peter 1:3 that God has already given you everything you need for life and godliness. Not just some things, but everything you need. We need to start reading, believing and confessing the truth. This CD helps you to do just that!

What we speak has power and therefore when we confess the truth contained in the word of God, power is released and the word brings life. Speak life and truth into your circumstances and let's see God do a miracle! **Also available to download from iTunes and other online platforms.**

Speak...Declare the Truth: Vol 2

Do you know you are loved? Do you realise you are valued? Do you understand you are special? So many of us struggle with confidence, our self-image and our mental ability to believe we are worthy. We don't value ourselves and therefore we cannot see how anyone else will value us. Do you know God delights in you and celebrates you? Do you realise that he sings songs of joy and delight over you? Do you struggle with the ability to see a joyful future full of hope? God not only believes in you but he has wonderful plans and purposes for your life. Who are you listening to? Who are you believing? We need to listen to the truth of the word of God rather than listening to the lies of the enemy.

There is power in the spoken word, so read, believe and confess the truth and see your circumstances and your life change for the better. **Also available to download from iTunes and other online platforms.**

All meditation cds are available direct from ngm at:

www.ngm.org.uk, www.nancygoudie.com

Other Products

Bible Reading Planners

A superb way of systematically reading through the Bible in one or two years.

Wholehearted - by Leanne Goudie

Wholehearted is a 30-day interactive devotional written by Leanne Goudie and packed full of encouragements, scriptures and space to journal. So many women go through life struggling to embrace their God given identity and worth, so Wholehearted was written to encourage and equip women in their everyday lives.

Throughout the book there is space to journal and write, allowing you to process anything that arises from reading the encouragement given each day. This is your devotional and your space to process, so take it at your own pace and enjoy the journey of living your life. Grab your copy now! **Only available on Amazon Kindle.**

Rooted - by Leanne Goudie

Rooted was created to help you delve deeper into what it is to truly trust God and encourage you to look at how you can live a life of complete faith in Him. Throughout there is space for you to journal and process anything that arises from reading the encouragement given each day. This is your devotional and your space, so take it at your own pace and embrace the journey of becoming more and more 'Rooted' in your faith!

One Woman's Guide to Life - Zoe Wickham

At the time of writing this book I am 43 years old. I haven't lived all my years but I feel I have lived enough, and learned some life lessons the hard way, so I want to share them with others. My heart is that you will find freedom in these pages, you will be free to express who you were born to be, you will discover it's not too late to change things no matter what age you are, you will learn to take care of yourself and learn also that it's okay not have all the answers. I have read a lot of self-help books (there's nothing wrong with them) in the journey of trying to improve myself, but this isn't one of those. This is an honest account from a wife, a mum, a woman who has lived her first 40 plus years and wants to share with you some of the highs and lows to help you to find balance, happiness and joy in life and that you might learn to live life more fully!

NGM Worship - Unbreakable Love

Unbreakable Love featuring the beautiful vocals of Leanne and Esther. This is a great ep with some fantastic new songs, plus a re-release of the track Heal Our Nation from Heartbeat. Do make sure you grab your copy for yourself and for your family/friends!

Also available to download from iTunes and other online platforms.

All of these products are available direct from NGM at: www.ngm.org.uk, www.nancygoudie.com

NANCY GOUDIE CONTACT DETAILS:

Should you wish to contact Nancy,
then you can write to her at:

nancy@nancygoudie.com

The NGM Trust,
Caedmon Complex,
Bristol Road,
Thornbury, BS35 3JA

Facebook: Nancy Goudie
Twitter: @nancygoudie
Instagram: @nancygoudie
YouTube: Nancy Goudie – NGM Trust

If you wish to find out more about anything in the book
or request prayer you can call: 01454 414880

For more information on Nancy and all she is doing
visit www.nancygoudie.com